Protect the World

Protect the World from Coronavirus: A Collection of Poems

BY ACHIER DENG AKOL

With contributors Amou Tiit Akol Tiit, Lindsey Carver, Phoebe Osariemen Nkechinyere Brobbey, Roby Shamas, Seun Tolani, and Tanesha Carson-Pedley

ISBN: 9798699607723

We dedicate this book to key workers who sacrifice their lives to protect people from COVID-19 and children orphaned by COVID-19 to motivate and support them.

Proceeds from this book will go to aid needy children orphaned by the COVID-19 pandemic.

Table of Contents

Introduction

A new coronavirus, COVID-19, caused a pandemic that attacked our world in 2020, leading to numerous deaths and massive economic crises. Without a specific vaccine or therapy, the focus is on prevention by washing and wiping hands, wearing face coverings, and social distancing. With vaccination well underway, there is light at the end of the tunnel.

Essential workers worldwide struggled to stamp the spread of COVID-19. Full and tier lockdowns helped to stop the spread of the virus, but social and economic deprivation pains were endured.

A lot of key workers put themselves at risk, prompting worldwide applause for them in gratitude. This book aims to supplement these appreciations with poetry. The poems extend to key workers fighting behind the scenes, such as morticians, embalmers, and cleaners.

We organized the poems into three eras: the brighter days that occurred precorona, the new normal that is occurring during corona, and the predicted new world post–COVID-19, which is likely to be much bleaker or, at the very least, more complex than triumphant. Every poem is heart touching. The title of this book comes from the poem "Protect the World," written from the perspective of a one-year-old child, which makes a plea for everyone to protect the world. Considering that COVID-19 can destroy our planet, this plea is in place.

In the course of writing this book, a number of fellow health workers, doctors, midwives, health attendants, and social workers voluntarily offered to contribute some poems. We all wanted to do something beyond shedding our tears for the victims of COVID-19.

We hope the book will motivate and raise funds to support children orphaned by COVID-19. As the book is intended to benefit children financially, the audience should have been children and not adults. However, the essential workers fighting the coronavirus at the front lines are adults to whom most of the scenarios, where the poems are derived, are applicable. The parents of the children sacrificed their lives to protect us. We should, in turn, take care of their loved ones. We may weep for the victims of COVID-19, but tears alone will not help them. We should do something more beyond tears, however little!

—Achier Deng Akol

Era One:
Brighter Days—before Corona

We Are the World, Aren't We Still?

BY ACHIER DENG AKOL

When famine hit Africa
And earthquakes struck Haiti,
Michael Jackson
And Lionel Richie
Said, "Oh! No!
We must do something."
Their voices erupted
Vibrantly:

"There comes a time
When we heed a certain call,
When the world must come together as one.
There are people dying…"

"We are the world.
We are the children.
We are the ones who make a brighter day,
So let's start giving…"

Michael Jackson may be gone.
Kenny Rogers has passed on.
Gone are their bodies;
Aren't their voices alive?

Along with more stars,
They sang
"We Are the World"
And saved a lot of lives.

Viruses are more rampant.
Global collapse is imminent.
Let's sing another version:
"We are the world, aren't we still?"

Parents Will Have Some Time to Breathe

BY ACHIER DENG AKOL

The sun has risen,
Little ones still enjoying their sleep.
"Wake up, kids.
It's time to go to school."

A school bag, displaced;
The search for socks, a nightmare;
The pencil box, nowhere to be seen.
Some have not completed their homework.

Breakfast is ready to go.
Children are running around the house
Gathering all they can.
The clock is ticking.

"Oops! I have stained my school uniform."
"Mummy, why do I have to go to school?"
A school taxi is about to arrive.
The excitement for school has built up.

School doors open;
Parents will have some time to breathe.
Children pave the way for a bright future.

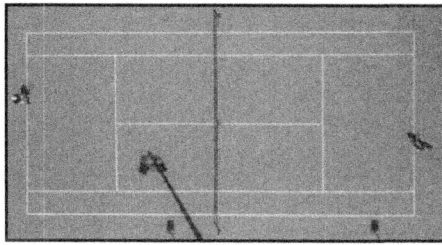

You Are All Welcome to Kuajok
A POEM FOR SERENA WILLIAMS BY ACHIER DENG AKOL

What you placed on your parietal
Is not only a Wimbledon crown
Or merely a lucrative tennis medal;
It's more than golden brown.
It's the joy of every tennis lover,
The victory of any sports player,
The prize of a relentless achiever,
A reward of a very hard worker.

With your crown placed head-on
And your arms saying, "I rule,"
Your name could be Nyanthon,
A daughter of the fiercest bull.

An offspring of the Kush fighters;
A *candace* of the Nubian archers.

You fully epitomized the toiling womenfolk
And lifted them to the top of the globe

With a powerful spirit and enormous hope.
Oracene Price and Richard Williams,
Yetunde, Lyndrea, Isha, and Venuce,
Candace Nyanthon Serena Williams,
The world number one in tennis.

You are all welcome to Kuajok.

Why Can't Every Day Be a Birthday?

BY ACHIER DENG AKOL

"When is my birthday coming, Mum?"
"It's five months away, darling!"
"Oh! I see!
I wish the clock would tick faster."

"What will I have for my birthday, Dad?"
"What would you like to have?"
"A portrait of myself, Daddy."
"Umm, that may be tricky to get."

A phone call rings at McDonald's.
Parents booked a birthday party for kids.
A birthday gift is already packed;
Invitation cards are all dispatched.

The moment is about to arrive.
The birthday girl is well dressed,
Her hair beautifully braided overnight,
Light-flashing shoes put on.

Alesha welcomes friends with gifts.
"Happy birthday to you,"
The McDonald's room roars.
Ooh! The candle lights go out.
Wow! Alesha cuts the Peppa Pig cake.
Mmm! The flavors are delicious.
Pop! The balloons light up the hall.

Why can't every day be a birthday?

Heart of Gold, Sponsor Me
BY ACHIER DENG AKOL

A stomach is deceivable;
Fill it with anything,
And it will feel satiated.

Don't pack it
With pieces of glass;
They'll kill you faster.

A jug full of water,
A bunch of leaves,
A thumb of mud
Can mask hunger
And spare a tear.

Beg on a roadside
For a dime!
No! I won't shame
My land and people,
Though I am blind.

All I need is one,
One fishing net,
To catch a fish.
One plough
To dig the soil.
One pillow
To rest my head.
One cottage
To hide my skin.
One sponsor
To support me.
One God
To protect my soul.

I need no tears;
They won't suffice.
If nothing else,
Give me cheers
To encourage me.

One apple a day
Will do me good.
Where can I get it?
To the poverty-stricken me,
An apple is a dream!

My eyes are blind;
I see with my heart.
Somewhere there,
On this planet,
Is a heart of gold.
Is that you?

All I need is one.
All I need is you.
Sponsor me.

La corona—What a Beautiful Name!
A POEM FOR THE WORD *CORONA* BY ACHIER DENG AKOL

A gaseous envelope
Of the sun and stars.
A glow around a conductor
At high potential.
A circle of light
Around the sun and moon,
Diffraction by water droplets.

A part of the body
Resembling a crown.
A cup of a daffodil flower.
A trumpet of a narcissus flower.

A chandelier in a church.
A broad part of a cornice.
A long, straight-sided cigar.
A Latin-Spanish name for a crown.

La corona—
What a beautiful name!

The 2019 Economy Was Better

BY ACHIER DENG AKOL

Who would top the billionaires' list next year?
Zuckerberg, Bezos, Gates, or Ortega?
Which impoverished continent will step up a gear?
Antarctica, Africa, Asia, or South America?

The world economy was booming;
Many planes filled the sky;
The aviation industry was flourishing;
The Primark trade was sky high.;

The lockdown hit businesses hard.
Thomas Cook shut its doors.
Three bank branches had red cards
In New Jersey for underperforming.

Despite the dilemma of Brexit,
The UK economy faced no recession.
The UK would from Europe exit,
Brexiteers set to win the election.

The future looked bright.
The unemployment rate was low.
Sterling held tight.
The economy seemed to glow.

The 2019 economy was better.

A Wedding of Weddings: Love Above All Loves
BY ACHIER DENG AKOL

When love is so deep,
It crosses all boundaries.

"How deep is your love?"
Calvin Harris and Disciples ask.
"Is it like the ocean?"
They add.

Your love, Prince Harry
And Meghan Markle,
Is deeper than an ocean.
No word can describe it.

Billions of people
Watched your wedding.
Thousands of guests
Attended your receptions.
Numerous fans lined up
To have a glance at you.

A wedding of weddings;
Love above all loves.

Leaving an empty chair for your mum,
The late Diana, Princess of Wales,
Was undoubtedly a tribute so touching!
A move that brought me tears of joy.
A gesture that touched millions of hearts.

Harry and Meghan, that chair was not empty.
Princess Diana occupied it in spirit.
She attended and enjoyed your wedding.
She was proud of both of you.

When your mum visited St. Joseph's Primary School
In Holborn in Greater London during the early 1990s,
She walked straight ahead and held the hands of Deng,
The only lowborn black African child in that class.
A move my son Deng Akol Sr. has never forgotten.
Extreme joy and pride for a dream come true.
A tender touch from Diana, the Princess of Wales.
For years he has continued to dream happily about this.
Now he is one of the millions whose heart was touched
By your tribute of leaving one chair empty for your mum.

A corona-free wedding before 2020:
Terrific, fabulous, one in a trillion.

Prince Harry and Meghan Markle,
Your breathtaking walk on the aisles,
Your wedding kiss so romantic
In front of St. George's Chapel.
The choice of the Windsor Castle,
Stunning scenery all around.

The fabulous lemon elderflower cake.
The lily of the valley flowers.
The blooms of forget-me-nots and more.
Meghan's natural beauty.
The Clare Waight Keller wedding dress.
The Stella McCartney reception dress.
The Queens Mary's bandeau tiara.
Awesome selections so gorgeous,
Every ground you stepped on
Vibrated with extreme joy.

The stride of the bride and groom
In the distinctive royal wagon.
Every spectator you glanced at
felt deeply honored and touched.

A wedding of weddings;
Love above all loves.

I Am All Yours, Darling—Let's Zero Distance

BY ACHIER DENG AKOL

What a dance floor! So packed;
When one scratches one's bum,
One accidentally fondles another person.

The music is loud
With a romantic rhythm.
"Dance all night long,"
In the words of Lionel Ritchie.

Every pair, lover to lover,
With zero distance between them.
Touching breast to chest,
Front to front.

Feeling the romantic pulsations
Of each other's heartbeats,
Excitement at the peak,
Wetness at the lips.

Bodies shaking,
Pulses racing,
Touches so sweet,
Feeling on top.

Hold me tight, darling.
I am about to fall down
In absolute excitement.
What a pity that dance floors
Lack beds.

I am all yours, darling.
The basement is open;
Enter if you can.
Enter! Enter! Enter!
Don't stop outside;
Do it while we dance.
I am all yours, darling.
All yours, all yours.

No air should flow,
No water can trickle
Between you and me
When we zero distance.
On the dance floor

Dance like that
With another,
And I promise
I will kill you.
You are all mine.
I won't share
A piece of you
With anyone else.

A dance
Of a lifetime.
A hug
In a trillion.
Romance
Beyond imagination.
A moment
To cherish.
A time
To remember.
A love flows
Between you and me.

I am all yours, darling
Let's zero distance

What Happens Next?

BY ACHIER DENG AKOL

I knew one day
I would meet you, my sweetheart.
I prayed and prayed
To find you, honey.

My friends who started
To enjoy sex before me
Thought I was a fool,
Wasting my time and life away.
They thought I would not find you—
My dream man that needs all of me,
Not just a little piece of me.

Now we are in a honeymoon suite
In the romantic city of Rome.

Come on, darling,
No more life to waste.
I know I am nervous,

Having not done it before.
Come on; come on; come in.
Show me how it feels
For the first time in my life.
Gentle, please, don't hurt me.
Take me now; have me all.

He is holding my hands.
Is that where it begins?
Hugging me tightly.
How can I breathe?
Kissing me hungrily.
A step before sex?
Touching me down there.
What happens next?

Era Two:
New Normal—during Corona

COVID-19

BY LINDSEY CARVER

What does this mean?
A pandemic of destruction
Waiting for our instruction.

COVID-19.

What does this mean?
Social distancing and isolation.
Loneliness and self-reflection.

COVID-19.

What does this mean?
Changes we need to make to our lives.
Changes that will help us survive.

Applause Day
BY LINDSEY CARVER

Thursday is Applause Day.
At 8:00 p.m. we gather and greet,
Everyone standing in the street.

We cheer and we clap,
Bang saucepans and tap.

We are happy, and we smile
At one another from afar;
We show gratitude to all the key workers.

Thursday is Applause Day

Protection

BY LINDSEY CARVER

Coronavirus has come to haunt us.
What can we do to survive this?

Prepare to listen to our instructions:
Work together as a nation;
Social distance from one another;
Two meters is the rule;
Face masks to fight the infection;
Live in sterile environments
For our protection.

Coronavirus

BY LINDSEY CARVER

Coronavirus.

We care.

We provide.

We reflect.

We survive.

Behind the Mask

BY LINDSEY CARVER

Smiles.
Sadness.
Hiding emotion.
Dehydration.
Unable to read facial expressions.
Unable to show compassion.

Look into our eyes.
A story to tell:
Smiles and sadness
Behind the mask.

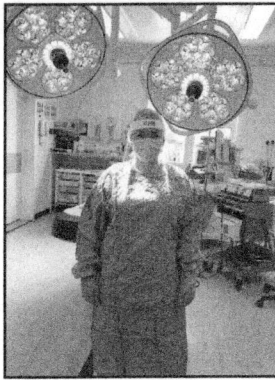

PPE

BY LINDSEY CARVER

We need masks.
We need aprons.
We need visors.
We need survival.

We need support.
We need time.
We need reflection.
We need protection.

We need uniforms.
We need scrubs.
We need hats.
We need PPE.

NHS Heroes

BY LINDSEY CARVER

NHS heroes,
Frontline survivors
Taking chances with their lives,
Providing care while in disguise.
PPE is their protection
To prepare to care for their nation.
Exhaustion follows, but they soldier on
Until this pandemic is completely gone.

A New Normal

BY LINDSEY CARVER

"A new normal," that's what they say
Is what to expect with every new day.

Social hugging and kissing is no more.
No more shopping as before.

How can we look ahead and plan for our future
When our lives are awaiting a new structure?

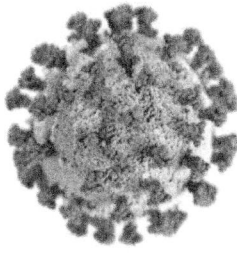

An Unwanted Visitor

SEUN TOLANI

It arrived with no warning,
Invisible but powerful.

Terror was in its army.
Force, its weapon.

Agony, its accomplice.
Trampling the strong and the weak.

The rich and the poor.
The young and the old.

No respect for boundaries.

Wherever it goes,
Destruction ensues.

Will We Ever Know?

BY ACHIER DENG AKOL

Will we ever know
Where COVID-19 originated?
Will they ever show
How coronavirus emanated?

Politicians may point fingers
Suspiciously against each other.
They may raise their whiskers,
Exchanging words so bitter.

Will we ever know
Whether they threw corona
From somewhere to China?
Whether it was grown
In Wuhan and blown?

The answer isn't
From media microphones.
It may have risen
From genuine microscopes.

Some allege it's from a Wuhan lab.
Others say it's from a wet animal market.
Some believe it's a human-made weapon.
Others assert it is zoonotic from a rodent.

Will we ever know?

Go Away, Coronavirus!

BY ACHIER DENG AKOL

Some asked the government
To rescue a multibillion airline,
While most on furlough lament
Only Amazon is thriving so beautifully.

It threatened multibillion businesses;
The aviation industry is on a standstill.
It crumbled the hospitality industry;
Every small business has fallen downhill.

Go away!

When billionaires worry,
And the poor sob and cry;
When we all feel so sorry,
And our planes do not fly.

This COVID-19 disaster,
The worst that has ever been.
This economic destroyer,
A deadly virus that is so mean.

Go away!

You caused pain in every way
And sent our economy astray.
You suspended children's educations
And affected every existing nation.
You ruined all our general health
And inflicted suffering and death.

Go away, Coronavirus!

Coronavirus, You Will Not Win!
From a Baby Whose Mother Died of Coronavirus after Giving Birth

BY ACHIER DENG AKOL

Never will I taste your milk.
Never will I feel your tender touch.
Never will I hear your loving voice.

Never will I feel the joy of your hug.
Never will I be soothed by your soft voice.
Never will I enjoy a nap on your lap.

Mummy, I love you.
Mummy, may God take care of you.
Coronavirus, you will not win.

I will live and be healthy.
I will rise from the ashes of your doom.
I will survive and follow in your footsteps.

Coronavirus, you will not win!

Coronavirus or Not, the Carer Has Won
BY ACHIER DENG AKOL

Blue or red, America is one.
Blue or white, the Nile is one.
Clear or cloudy, the sky is one.
Half or full, the moon is one.
Head or toe, the body is one.
Atria or ventricles, the heart is one.
Black or white, the skin is one.
Cerebrum or cerebellum, the brain is one.
Biden or Trump, the choice is one.

Pennsylvania or Florida, the states run.
Rich or poor, the voters span.
Postal or personal, the votes stand.
Biden or Trump, the winner is one.
Loser or winner, the election is done.
Won or slumped, the outcomes stun.
Coronavirus or not, the carer has won
Angela or Kamala, a woman can.
Democrats or Republicans, now coplan.

Sinking

BY PHOEBE OSARIEMEN NKECHINYERE BROBBEY

An underlying tone.
A constant presence.
In moments I feel it swell.
My heart races.
Sweat drips.
Thoughts fly.
And then
It eases.
But it does not depart entirely.

It is always there.
Lurking.
Lingering.
Ready to surface.

Others feel it too.

I notice it in the mirror
As I try to hide the circles that show
The nights are not being kind.

I notice it as I speak,
Each word not so carefully planned,
Wondering if the receiving ears
Are hearing the words or the SOS code.

Is this how it is supposed to feel
In a strange time?

I feel fine.
I am not fine.
My mind feels not mine.

And when things return,
If we ever go back,
What do I do with this feeling?

An extra check.
A **N**od instead of what I want to say.
In these e**X**treme circumstances,
Are we all merely wa**I**ting
For some **E**xtreme release?
Maybe just **T**o say
You are still here.
ANXIETY

Behind Window Glass

BY ACHIER DENG AKOL

Not a prisoner
Behind bars.
Never a criminal
Within a cell.

Locked away from love,
At the edge of my grave,
Behind window glass,
Thanks to coronavirus.

Impervious without flow;
Insensitive without sound;
Vacant without relatives;
A glass without nerves.

Can't feel their touch,
Can't enjoy their love
Behind window glass
When they visit me.

Away in a nursing home,
Shaking from loneliness
Behind window glass.
May go without a goodbye.

Oh! Grandma!

BY ACHIER DENG AKOL

Don't cry.
Don't worry.
We're with you.

Locked away,
We know.
Frail every day.
Oh no,
They say.
From corona
You're isolated.
From a killer
You're protected.

Don't cry.
Don't worry.
Residents dying, too,
In large numbers
From corona

In nursing homes.
Threatened grandma,
You're
Frightened grandma.
You may be.

Don't cry.
Don't worry.
The virus
Will go.
Key workers
Will win
The lockdown,
Will lift
Our doors,
Will reopen.
Don't cry.
Don't worry.
We're with you.
Oh! Grandma!

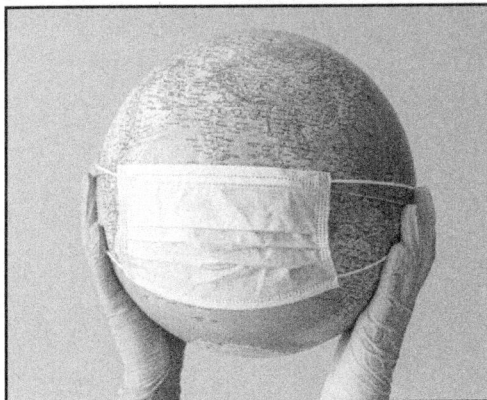

Happy Birthday, Colonel Tom

BY DR. ACHIER DENG AKOL AND DR. TANESHA CARSON-PEDLEY

Your kind thought to help others.
Your walk at ninety-nine to fight coronavirus.

Heroes like you should live longer.
Kind hearts like yours should beat forever.

Once a soldier, always a fighter.
You inspired us in the NHS
To conquer this killer.

Colonel Tom Moore,
You deserve more,
More than cheers,
More than one hundred years.

Happy Birthday, Colonel Tom Moore,
From George Eliot Hospital NHS Trust, labor ward staff.

This Devotedness, I Promise You

BY ACHIER DENG AKOL

Never did I know
You would leave me
Without a chance for me
To tell you goodbye.

When you were in critical condition,
I called you on FaceTime.
I sent you a tweet.
I phoned you on WhatsApp.
They were better than nothing
But not enough.

When the hospital called
To say you were gone,
I offered to go to there
To hold and hug you,
To kiss you, my husband.
Prepared to catch corona,
I was not allowed.

The shock of losing you
While I was far from your side,
The deep sorrow that followed,
The negative impact on me
Will never go away
Whatever I do.

If you were dying at home,
I would have been by your side
To hold your hands
And say goodbye.
During your last hour,
Home was better.

I should have respected
Your advance directive
Not to take you to hospital
And allowed you to die at home,
But I had hoped you might be treated.

In your absence,
I will continue
To raise our kids
As your legacy.
I will carry on
My mission
As your wife.

I am still young.

My beauty will prevail.
Men will run after me
To replace you.
I will reject them.
I will remain yours forever.
This devotedness I promise you.

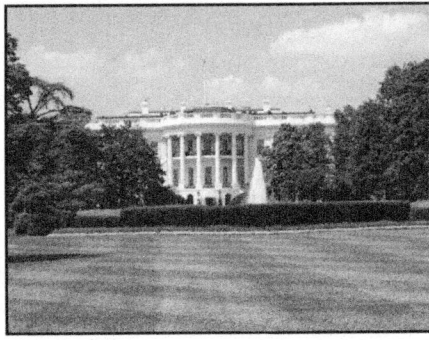

Put the Blame Aside; Save Lives
BY ACHIER DENG AKOL

The coffins in Italy.
The deaths in Spain.
The tears in China.
The cries in Africa.
The riots in America.

Put the blame aside.

It's a global disaster.
It spares no nation.
It attacks everybody,
President or servant,
Young or old.

COVID-19
Is a pandemic.
Coronavirus,

Facing academicians,
Is a terrible killer,
Severely pneumonic.

Stop quarrelling
Over the USA versus China.
Fight the virus.
Step aside
From politics.
Put the blame aside;
Save lives.

It's beyond Imagination
BY ACHIER DENG AKOL

Easter has never come and gone
Without being celebrated in churches.

We shouldn't keep children in lockdown at home,
Unable to attend school all over the world.

No one should stop Christians
From attending masses on Sundays.

No authority should prohibit Muslims
From praying in mosques on Fridays.

Restaurants, bars, pubs, and cinemas,
Parks, saloons, clubs, and stadiums,
Passenger flights, and crowded festivals,
They were never barred worldwide.

It's beyond imagination.

Family members not allowed to visit one another,
Prisoners released before parole,
Funeral attendants limited to five,
Wedding parties not permitted,
Birthday parties restricted to
Only members of a household.
Shop for only food and medicines;
Exercise for only one hour a day;
Don't mention discos and gyms.

It's beyond imagination.

Stay Safe

BY ACHIER DENG AKOL

Feet greet;
No handshake.

Bump push;
The door opens.

Elbow-pull
The window closed.

Wink-blink
A lover afar.

Social distance
In a queue.

Toe clit
On a bed.

Mask to mask,
Not lip to lip.

Back to back,
Not front to front.

New styles;
New vocabulary.

Stay safe.

Angels Have Ears

BY ACHIER DENG AKOL

We, the living, think
We have ears,
The dead do too.
Angels have ears.

The whispers we make
On dark nights in bed,
The gossip we pour
Behind closed doors
Are heard by others.
Angels have ears.

When we clap for our loved ones,
They may not understand,
May not have anticipated our nice gesture.
They are no longer in their coffins;
They have risen to heaven above
For all the good they have done.

The loved ones we lost from corona
Fighting day and night to protect us
Are no longer the surgeons or cleaners,
The nurses, midwives, caregivers we knew.
They are more than good servants;
They are now glorious angels in heaven.

As their coffins move in front of us
In hearses crowned with flowers,
Tears flow over our shocked faces
Onto our hospital uniforms, like they once wore.
The farewell claps roar in the air
From the hands of their colleagues,
A warm farewell like no other.
The corona battle they succumbed to,
We will continue it by all means
Till the dawn of ultimate victory.

Angels have ears.

Let Us Hope They Will Be Okay

BY ACHIER DENG AKOL

When they sit meters apart on TV,
The little ones are confused.
"Don't they like each other anymore?"
When customers queue meters apart,
The passengers in public transport sit afar.
The little ones wonder, "Why?"

"Why are we speaking to Grandma
Outside through a glass window?"
"Why is the aunty we miss
Talking to us from a distance?"
"What is happening, Mummy?

"Why is our trip canceled
To Disneyland Paris?"
"Why are we suddenly stopped
From going to school to learn?"
"Why is it now a crime
To go and pray in church or mosque?"

"Why can't we go to enjoy a meal
At McDonald's or Kentucky Fried Chicken?"
"Have we done anything wrong?"
"What's happening, Daddy?"

We fight back the tears
When our kids wonder,
When they ask questions
So sensitive, so deep,
So curious, so complex.

To answer, "COVID-19" simply sparks more.
"Why 'nineteen' when we have never heard of 'one, two,
three...eighteen?'"

The little ones are confused and profoundly affected.
Let us hope they will be OK in the time to come.

Corona Is Enough! We Do Not Need More!

BY ACHIER DENG AKOL

The thunder that still strikes,
The fires that still burn,
Malaria that still kills—
Isn't corona enough?

Why step on our necks
When we have been attacked
By a dangerous coronavirus
That stops us from breathing?
Isn't corona enough?

Why ignite riots
In cities threatened
By a serious killer?
Isn't corona enough?

Is this the time
To capture Tripoli?
Is this the day

To advocate terror?
Do you still need to raid cattle
And massacre innocent children?
Isn't corona enough?

Oh, Lord! Please!
No more earthquakes.
No more volcanoes.
No more hurricanes.
No more avalanches.
No more bush fires.
No more tsunamis.
No more killings.
Corona is enough!
We do not need more!

All Lives Matter!

BY ACHIER DENG AKOL

Listen to Michael Jackson.
It doesn't matter
If you are black or white.
You aren't better
If you are dark or light.

George Washington of Popes Creek,
George Bush Sr. of Milton,
George Kongor of South Sudan,
George Floyd of Houston—
All Georges, all gorgeous, all equal.

All lives matter!

Catholic Irish or Anglican English,
American white or African black,
Do not treat people like rubbish;
Do not kneel on someone's neck.

We all fight for our nations,
Lowborn black or royal white.
We rise above any situations
When national interests overlap.

We all score goals
When we play soccer.
We do tactical rolls
And score goals.

With corona in our tracks
And you on our necks,
When one says, "I can't breathe! Please!"
The other person should kindly release.

Black lives matter!

A Lifetime of Worries—Am I Safe from Corona?

BY ACHIER DENG AKOL

The hospital car park,
The hospital on-call room,
The mattress I am lying on,
The quilt over my body,
The pillow under my head,
Following a night on call—
Am I surely safe?

What about other fomites?
The toilet seat I am sitting on,
The flush button I am pressing.
Are they free of corona?

The doctor's office,
The changing room door,
The labor ward uniform,
The theater shoes I am wearing,
The hospital computer desktop,
The Sonicaid fetal doppler,

The outpatient clinic facilities,
The portable ultrasound scanner,
The staff kitchen utilities—
Who else has used them?

A virus I can't see,
Like whales deep in a sea,
A killer that's invisible,
A germ that seems invincible—
Where is it now?

A lifetime of worries—
Am I safe from corona?

Fight Together; We Will Beat This

BY ACHIER DENG AKOL

You think you are a harsh killer.
You believe you are invincible.
Wait for us, the key workers.
We will defeat you.
You will be our target.
You will never forget.

We will wash our hands
With disinfectant brands.
We will use gloves.
We will always social distance.
Universities will create a vaccine.
Scientists shall discover treatment.

We will fight together
Like a solid block.
We'll protect one another
As a mighty rock.

All we need
Are PPEs
And indeed
The respirators.

Fight together;
We will beat this.

We Will Fly to the Moon When This Is All Over

BY ACHIER DENG AKOL

The hugs we have missed,
The opportunities we lost,
Lovers we have not kissed,
Holidays we wanted most—
Oh! We missed them!

Relaxation on the beach,
Entertainment on the stage,
Message all over the body,
Live excitement at a stadium—
We'll again swim in happiness!

Sunshine wasting away
With no one exercising,
A wedding party astray
With none to participate—
We need our lives back!

Our hopes may flicker.
The rainbows will glitter.
Corona will go soon.
Hang on, my lover.
We will fly to the moon
When this is all over,
And corona will be over!

Clap for Us Too

BY ACHIER DENG AKOL

We aren't trivial,
Not rock bottom.
Like nurses and doctors,
We are important too.

Top-class
Environmental service providers.
Not bottom-class
National health system workers.

In a corona pandemic
Defined by cleanliness,
How can we be bottom class
And not among the top class?

Collecting bins,
Clearing dirt,
Wiping fomites,
Changing linens,

Arranging curtains,
Dressing COVID-19 patients,
Washing their dead bodies.

Clap for us too.
Oh! Public appreciators
Value what we do.
Ye government leaders
Include us as beneficiaries,
Reward us with necessities.

Top-class key workers,
Not bottom-class cleaners.

Clap for us too.

Recognize Others behind the Scenes

BY ACHIER DENG AKOL

Behind locked doors,
Inside closed restaurants,
Charity cooks are busy
Preparing food for the NHS
Behind the scenes.

Farmers producing food,
Trailers delivering goods
To a hospital venue,
Not for revenue.

Taxi drivers
Risking their lives
Transporting ill passengers
Whatever their blights.

Crematoria staff and embalmers,
Funeral directors and social workers,
All working extremely hard
For their societies' pride.

Lawyers enforcing laws
To protect communities,
Police confronting outlaws
To help prevent fatalities.

Yes! Value politicians
Offering public briefs;
Don't forget morticians
Tackling shocking griefs.

Recognize others
Behind the scenes.

Breakthrough

BY ACHIER DENG AKOL

Imagine all the people that died from corona,
All over the world, rising from the dead.

"Come back," the Lord said,
And John Smith put up a fight,
Surviving from a deep coma
In the film called *Breakthrough*,
Defying all human imagination,
His mother solemnly by his side,
His frightened father there for him,
His brother, a pastor, standing by him,
Colleagues, mates, a prayer group,
His dream mentors who he aspires to be,
A caring rescue and medical team.

The voices of the choir,
The romantic sobs and cries
Of his loving girlfriend,
The spirit of Michael Jordan,

The candles everyone lit,
The endless sound of his mum,
The affectionate touch of his hands,
He defied medical science.
He came back from the dead
By the will of the Almighty,
Via the power of love.

Imagine all the dead victims
Of the COVID-19 pandemic and more
Making a miraculous breakthrough
Like John Smith, son of Joyce Smith.
The tears of sorrow we shed
Will turn into tears of joy.
Those we clapped farewell to
Will rise again victoriously.
The six-week-old orphan
Will taste their mother's milk again!
Breakthrough.

Love Wins
BY ACHIER DENG AKOL

Loveless you are,
The devilish you,
Killer of the weak,
Source of sorrow,
You will never win.

When we conquer you,
Dry eyes
Will all fill up
With tears of joy.

People without voices
Will develop sweet ones.
The blind among us
Will see with their hearts.

When you surrender,
We will march and gather.
We'll sing songs of victory.
We'll wave flags of liberty.

From anthems of nations
To psalms of religions,
From rhythms of romance
To verses of allegiance.

Stand by me;
Lean on me;
Love wins;
We'll all sing.

Love wins.

Princess Sofia, You're More than a Star

BY ACHIER DENG AKOL

From royal highness
To lowborn worker,
A wonderful princess
To a simple cleaner,
We salute you
Princess Sofia of Sweden.

A royal princess
With love in excess,
Lowering her royalty
To reduce mortality.

A heart so caring,
A lady so humble,
A royal so daring—
Corona will tumble.

Touching the heart
Of Sweden with hope,
Motivating all parts
Of the entire globe.

You have raised the bar
Of the anticorona campaign,
By all means above par,
For all nations to reign.

Princess Sofia of Sweden,
You are more than a star.

The World Was Gasping

BY ACHIER DENG AKOL

People held their breath
For Boris Johnson's health.
The UK Prime Minister
Caught a virus so sinister.

All eyes were open.
Don't ignore this virus.
The worst can happen.
It's a terrible menace.

Corona challenged the UK.
NHS was put in the spotlight.
People were frightened
About the PM's plight.

Imagine the worst thing.
What would the world think
About our health system,
About the United Kingdom?

From 10 Downing Street
To St. Thomas Hospital,
A dangerous virus to beat
In London, the capital.

Everyone prayed
For full recovery;
Key workers played
Roles in mastery.

The world was gasping.

Wish You Were Here

BY ACHIER DENG AKOL

We lost you on that horrible day of June 8.
A president so young, only fifty-five years old,
A liberator of the nation of Burundi,
Burundi's president, Pierre Nkurunziza.

Your willingness to give up power,
Your allegiance to your constitution,
Your acceptance of the people's will,
Your pride for your sovereign nation—
Wish you were here.

To welcome your wife back
From the country of Kenya,
Successfully treated from COVID,
She returned to find you dead.

To see if fellow skeptics would change:
Belarus's leader, Alexander Lukashenko;
Brazil's president, Jair Bolsonaro;
Tanzania's president, John Magufuli;

To see if you would do things better,
To follow the rest of the world,
To try a countrywide lockdown,
To adopt the social distancing strategy.

To give your wife a chance
To see you again,
To hold your hands,
To say goodbye.

Wish you fully recovered
For the pride of Africa.

Wish you were here,
Burundi's president, Pierre Nkurunziza.

Sir Tom Moore, the World Salutes You

BY ACHIER DENG AKOL

From out of sight
To spotlight,
Holding tight,
Walking right,
Military might,
Thinking bright,
Anticorona fight,
A royal knight.

An old man,
Two frail hands,
A thousand plans,
Thirty-three million pounds,
An NHS motivation
Beyond imagination—
A brave manhood
Deserved knighthood.

A well-earned ascendency,
A long-lasting legacy,
A fundraising supremacy,
A birthday celebration,
A charitable anniversary,
A brave elder in realty,
A risky walk for charity,
A distinction of humanity.

Sir Tom Moore,
The world salutes you.

A Wonderful World

BY ACHIER DENG AKOL

New Romeos and Juliets
Falling in love from a distance.

Painting post boxes blue in the UK,
A token of thanks to health staff
Battling coronavirus on the front lines.

Inundating centenarian Tom Moore in the UK
With an estimated 140,000 birthday cards.

Thousands of flamingos
Lighting up the lakes in Mumbai
With a shade of pink color.

Surviving champion Ava Henderson
Returning to surf in the sea,
Children returning to school.
Corona is losing.

The sun started to shine in Romford.
We took COVID-19 patients out of ICU,
The lovely warm weather with Vitamin D.

The iconic Rio de Janeiro statue illuminated,
An absolute tribute to medical workers.

The NY State Anderson river rainbow,
An Easter message of hope to residents.

The world's highest Himalayan mountains
Can now be seen the first time in decades,
Thanks to the reduction of air pollution.
Two little girls, Addyson and Lucy,
Distributing scarce toilet rolls to the elderly.
It's a beautiful world.

Every Little Gift Helps

BY ACHIER DENG AKOL

A little sip of water
When one is thirsty.
A small spread of butter
When one is hungry.

Sergio, Brian, and David
Teaching children via BBC.
The University of Oxford's efforts
To discover the COVID-19 vaccine.

The Royal Mail labeling envelopes
With happy-birthday wishes,
Drawings of the rainbows on windows,
Hope-for-all messages.

Many ways of helping out
A world of good hearts
During the lockdown throughout
To lift our spiritual parts.

An array of ideas for a gift
During and beyond the lockdown.
Valuable skills of thrift
To procure essential items around.

Every little gift helps.

With You in It, This World Is Better
A poem about celebrities with a heart of gold

BY ACHIER DENG AKOL

Little things make a difference;
Great things achieve more.
Every gift helps in abundance;
Helpers knock door to door.

Beauty Bank charity's £80,000
For items for the poor.
Run for Heroes' £75,000
For the NHS staff.

Donatella Versace's €200,000
For Milan coronavirus fighters.
NBA's Blake Griffith's $100,000
For Detroit workers.

NBA's Zion Williamson's $100,000
For New Orleans colleagues.
Professional footballers' thousands of pounds
For workers of suspended leagues.

Give one a penny;
It buys something tiny.
Give a thousand dollars;
It would be a lot better.

Great gifts achieve more.
The first step a child takes
Ultimately goes a long way.
You climb a mountain
By taking one at a time.

Los Angeles's Kylie Jenner raised $1 million
For hospital masks and staff uniforms.
The Golden State Warriors raised $1 million
To support workers in harmful situations.

Blake Lively and Ryan Reynolds's $1 million
To support food bank charities.
Legendary musician Dolly Parton's $1 million
For university research necessities.

NBA's Steph Curry and his wife Ayesha's $1 million
To feed children deprived of school meals.
Netflix's £1 million
For film crews that lost their job deals.

One as a figure appears minute;
It may be one but of high magnitude.
One cent may help anyway.
A million goes a long way.

The world's most parsimonious
Give zero million;

The outstanding magnanimous
Offer more than one million.

Rihanna's $2 million
For victims of domestic violence.
Oprah Winfrey's $10 million
For coronavirus relief assistance.
Leonardo DiCaprio's $12 million
For America's Food Fund.

Sir Tom Moore's £33 million
For NHS charitable institutions.
Lady Gaga's $35 million
For the World Health Organization.
Bill Gates's $50 million
To develop COVID-19 treatment.

Amazon's Jeff Bezos's $100 million
For Feeding America.
England Arts Council's £160 million
For organizations, freelancers, and artists.

The world is better
With you in it.
It shines brighter
With hearts lit.

This world is not mean;
It is full of angels,
People who are keen
To tackle all hurdles.

With you in it,
This world is better.

You Will Never Silence Our Voices

BY ACHIER DENG AKOL

Our voices emit encores
With the utmost quality.
We sing more and more
To overcome difficulties.

Sir Elton John's home concert
Entertaining people locked down.
Gaga, Lizzo, Billie Eilish, and Stevie Wonder
Staging a joint virtual music concert.

Ariana Grande, Taylor Swift, and Britney Spears
Donating funds directly to struggling fans.
Sir Tom Moore, Michael Ball, and the NHS band
Singing "You'll Never Walk Alone" with tears.

Corona or not,
We will sing and dance.
This virus will rot;
It will collapse and break.

You will never silence our voices,
You miserable coronavirus.

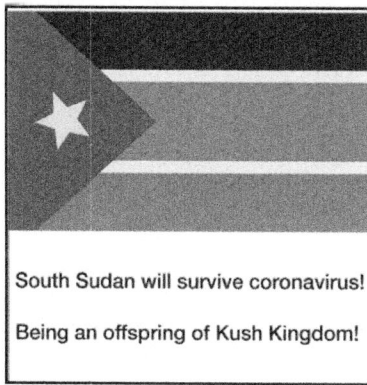

South Sudan will survive coronavirus!

Being an offspring of Kush Kingdom!

What Is Coronavirus? You Will Smash It!

BY ACHIER DENG AKOL

The Kingdom of Kush, the origin of South Sudan

Since 1640 BC, what pain have you not endured?
The wars of Egypt, Meroe, old Sudan, South Sudan,
Lasting tens, hundreds, thousands of years,
When people, resources, animals, perished.

What is a coronavirus? You will survive it!

Cush, the son of Ham, grandson of Noah,
The origin of the name of the Kingdom of Kush,
And its remnants of Equatoria, Waar Lol, Upper Nile regions,
Nubia, Nuba, Angesana, Darfur, and Abyei.

The Kush Kingdom: the mighty, wealthy land, the envy of all,
Enriched by the precious gold, copper, iron, uranium—
A land so fertile, able to grow fruits, vegetables, crops,
The wealth that attracted enemies near, far, here, there.

You fought and won many ancient battles, wars.
For decades you owned, controlled the Egypt dynasty.
For centuries you existed as the Kingdom of Kush.
Never gave up your rights, lands, cultures, existence.

What is coronavirus? You will conquer it!

Your tolerance in the past was followed by more war.
The contemporary armies of Anya-Nya and SPLA,
Where millions of youths, adults sacrificed their lives,
Enduring the agony of colonialism and neocolonialism.

What is coronavirus? You will overcome it!

Ancient kings like Priye, queens like Candace, and liberators
TopMac Miir, Gordon Muortat, Joseph Uduho, Fr. Saturnino
Joseph Lagu, Ager Gum, Deng Nhial, Kuac Kuac, Akol Ayai
John Garang, Kerbino Kuanyin, William Nyuon, Salva Kiir.

Heroes, heroines, of the Kingdom of Kush,
Countless liberators who fought merciless enemies
Without giving up and surrendering their land
Without turning their backs against their people.

What is coronavirus? You will defeat it.

What have you not suffered from before?
Hunger, famine, disease, slavery, misery,
Mosquitoes, snakes, thirst, drought, floods,
Tribalism, racism, nepotism, sectionalism.

What is coronavirus? You will beat it.

South Sudan, new Kush, land of the brave
My land of birth, motherland, fatherland,
Cry not, worry not, tremble not, surrender not,
My love, my life, my dream, my soul, my all.

What is coronavirus? You will smash it!

The Food You Give Motivates More than It Feeds
BY ACHIER DENG AKOL

Bride and groom Fiona and Adam Gordon
Donating their four hundred wedding meals to a hospital
After they canceled their wedding party.

Wagamama and Jamie Oliver giving cooking lessons
To support people and encourage them to carry on.

Pubs donating perishable food to ambulance and NHS staff
To keep their morale high as they combat COVID-19.

Liverpool FC, Everton, Aston Villa, Newcastle clubs
Donating food to food banks and large cash donations.

Restaurants preparing food behind closed doors
To deliver to the NHS staff and the elderly.

The food you give offers energy
To health staff working around the clock.

It maintains their everyday health.
It repairs their exhausted cells.

It lifts their spirits.
It shows you genuinely care.
It motivates them more
To fight and defeat corona.

The food you give
Motivates more than it feeds.

You Have No Chance to Win

BY ACHIER DENG AKOL

Attacked in every direction,
Keeping all the hands clean
With wipes and disinfectants,
You have no chance to win.

Free virtual counseling sessions
Helping neighboring countries,
Tooth Fairy and Easter Bunny
Putting smiling photos and names on PPE,
Alerting anyone trapped with a violent partner
About the risk of domestic violence,
Delivering nationwide speeches to instill hope,
Giving PE lessons to school children at home.

With multiple and diverse roles,
Motivational and professional tactics,
With heart-touching and inspiring calls
Deploying every formula in mathematics
To prevent you from infecting us.
Coronavirus, you have no chance to win

We, the Vulnerable, Can Disappoint Coronavirus

BY ACHIER DENG AKOL

Indeed, we are more vulnerable—
We, the elderly, age seventy and over—
But our resilience is indispensable.
We can survive corona forever.

One-hundred-four-year-old William Lapschie of the USA,
A 102-year-old woman from Genoa, Italy,
A 103-year-old woman in the Republic of Iran—
All recovered fully from COVID-19,
A testimony to their absolute resilience.

The very elderly tittle:
We cannot reject
The "vulnerable" label
We fully accept.

We say no
To our elimination
And shout, "Go!"
To support corona extinction.

We the vulnerable
Can disappoint coronavirus.

Motivation Sources

BY ACHIER DENG AKOL

A human mind is very creative.
It can generate any vital initiative.

Buying all the flowers in a florist's shop
To distribute to people freely,
Donating free PPE and respirators
To NHS staff working on the front lines.

Securing three hundred hotel rooms in London, UK,
For homeless people to isolate from corona,
Delivering a virtual mass in Rio de Janeiro
For COVID-19 victims worldwide.

Showing two penguins around the grounds
Of Shedd Aquarium in Chicago, USA,
Sharing an impromptu mass sing- and dance-along
To keep the spirits of housebound locals up.

Leaning out of windows to join together
And sing "You've Got a Friend."
Applauding health workers in all areas
To support and appreciate their efforts.

Offering to help shop
For people unable to leave homes,
Dedicating shopping hours
For the elderly and disabled.

The elderly playing a Hungry Hungry Hippos game
To entertain themselves.

These are the not kicks of dying horses.
They are motivation and survival sources.

They Sacrificed Their Profits to Fight the Coronavirus

BY ACHIER DENG AKOL

They suspended profitable business
To make breathing aids instead,
Stopped making luxurious cars
To manufacture more ventilators.
They used alcohol to make sanitizers,
Opened their hotels freely
To accommodate NHS staff.
They offered free virtual concerts
To fans in self-isolation,
Used perfume factories
To make disinfectant gels.
They gave discounts, treats, and more
To support all the medical staff,
Granted free hand gels and wipes
For vulnerable people over age sixty-five.
Artists painted free portraits
As tokens of appreciation to NHS staff.

They sacrificed their profits
To help fight the coronavirus.

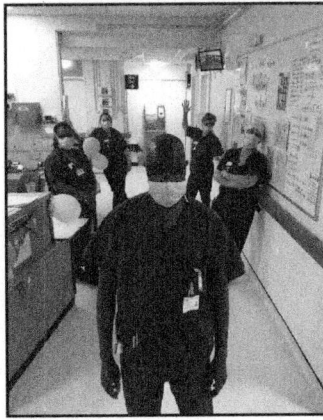

You Will Not Walk Alone

BY ACHIER DENG AKOL

You who sacrifices your life
To save us from coronavirus,
The health staff over the world,
The critical workers of all cadres.

You will not walk alone.

Like soldiers during the war
Who perished in the front line
Defending us against enemies,
It is now your turn to lead the war.

In hospital intensive care units,
In the accident emergency departments,
In maternity assessment and delivery suites,
In every hospital ward and theater,
You will not fight alone.
You will not walk alone.

The following poems, entitled "Dare I Ask You For a Donation?" "Wish I Did Not Wake Up," Where Will I Spend the Night?" and "Follow the Stars of the World," are grouped together as they all have the same speaker: an impoverished doctor in his sixties who manages a labor world and dedicates his time to caring for people with COVID-19. He experiences and understands the pains and agony of poverty and wishes to do something to alleviate this suffering from other people, especially children.

Dare I Ask You for a Donation?

BY ACHIER DENG AKOL

Forty years in the health service,
Breastfeeding research in Ratchaburi, Thailand,
Extensive service in South Sudan and Nigeria,
Over two decades serving the NHS in the UK,
Yet I cannot afford to buy a little cottage.

A master's degree in international community health,
A PhD degree in obstetrics and gynecology,
Numerous distinctions and prizes in health care,
A countless number of postgraduate certificates.

Risking my life to fight corona in the UK at a vulnerable
age—
Almost died in a road traffic accident driving to the hospital.
Unable to retire from work lest my blind brother starve,
Lest I can't care for my late-coming, one-year-old daughter.

"You are an angel on Earth for saving my life and my
twins"—

An example of so many beautiful cards I receive from patients.

"Thank you for teaching me how to perform caesarean sections"—

An example of commendations I obtain from junior colleagues.

"Thanks for saving our lives from COVID-19"—

The premier card we deservedly receive all over the world.

Thanks for recognizing our tireless efforts globally;

Thanks, too, for publicly applauding for us internationally.

You have motivated us to carry on fighting COVID-19,

Win against coronavirus and combat it by all means;

Yet we will continue to face unsurmountable poverty;

Yet I cannot afford to buy a little cottage

To move near the George Eliot Hospital in Warwickshire,

Where we continue to fight and will surely defeat coronavirus

Dare I ask you for a donation?

Wish I Did Not Wake Up

BY ACHIER DENG AKOL

The media lights were flashing.
I was in the spotlight for a while,
Like a president in a press conference,
A refugee
Who has won millions.

The wheel of the euro lottery was turning;
My numbers dropped down one after another;
I hit the jackpot of a hundred and thirty million;
I, a new millionaire, was added to the list.

I jumped up and down in ecstasy.
I trembled in front of the journalists.
I stammered when answering questions.
I worried about what would become of me in wealth.

Bought a luxurious house in Epson Down;
Boosted the accounts of my kids and grandkids;
Wired hundreds of thousands to my blind brother;
Donated thousands of pounds to orphans of COVID-19.

Then my eyes open from sleep
To find myself still sunk in poverty,
Sleeping roughly on a partially broken bed,
Hearing water from a broken tap.

I am still swimming in a sea of absolute poverty,
With eight children and six little grandchildren,
A helpless blind brother with three little children,
An age ticking away amid the threat of a pandemic.
I wish I did not wake up.

Where Will I Spend the Night?

BY ACHIER DENG AKOL

The agony of daily commutes
The working class have to survive,
Burton to Nuneaton to Burton,
A junior doctor for life.

Threats of road traffic accidents
Not at all an absolute deterrent.
How else would a family survive
Without work, without a salary?

The daily rounds in the wards,
Intensive clinics to conduct,
The surgeries to perform in theatre,
The hectic labor ward to manage.

When the clock strikes the end of the shift,
A routine walk to the car park
To find my car broken down,
A nightmare situation to address without funds.

Where would I sleep tonight
In a clinic alongside coronavirus?
Would I be safe there at all?
In a hospital hostel accommodation,
Where will I suddenly find twenty-seven pounds to pay?
Sit up all night in a library—
What will happen to my back?
Stay in the car all night long—
Would I not freeze in the car?
Go back to work when I am exhausted—
Would I not collapse in a prolonged shift?
Where will I spend the night?

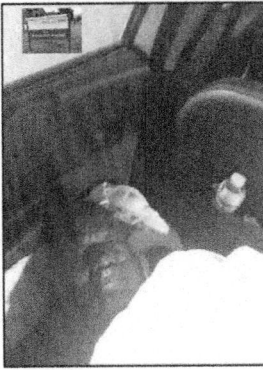

A snap
Of a health worker
A nap
Of a corona fighter

Dr Achier Deng Akol

Follow Stars of the World

BY ACHIER DENG AKOL

Some succeed;
Others recede
Due to sleep.
In slumber, you suffer;
Awake, you prosper.
Work hard when not asleep;
You will see more fruits ripe.

"Is that right?"
A poet wonders
"How many nights
Have I been awake
Toiling, thinking, weighing,
Sweating, rusting, suffering?"
Yet deeply sunk in the hole,
Immersed in its mud and soil,
The shaft of shameful poverty,
The rock bottom of misery,
Shedding tears of wretchedness,
Tears of miserable nothingness.

You roll around on a bed,
Hoping to grasp success.
You skip up and down,
Wishing to strike it rich.
You play the lottery for ages,
Dreaming of winning a jackpot,
Write one poem after another,
Believing someone will hold your hands
And pull you out of the pit of worthlessness.

Oh! Orphans!
Follow me not.
My steps of failure
Won't do you good.
They're steps of
Doom and gloom.
Follow me,
You will end up
In the streets.
You will fall
In deeper holes.
You will be a hero
Fighting coronavirus
But an unfortunate medical doctor,
A simple poetic author
Using poetry against corona,
Writing this book for charity
After hospital working hours.
No time to go home and rest,
Taking a nap at 3:59 a.m.
On the back seats
Of a secondhand car
In a hospital car park

After working hard
Almost the whole night,
Trying to raise funds
For COVID-19 orphans.
An attempt to provide help
For those who are needy.

Follow the steps of winners
Who brightened our dark world
With electricity,
Who sterilized milk
By pasteurization,
Who placed computers
On our laps,
Who occupied our fingers
With gadgets,
Who connected the world
With television,
Who eased communication
With telephones,
Who gave humans wings
With airplanes,
Who fought bacteria
With antibiotics,
Who distributed water
With pipes,
Who covered nakedness
With clothes,
Who prevented coronavirus
With simple measures,
Who changed the world with goodness.

Letter *A* stands for Apple computer,
Not apple fruit,

Thanks to Steve Jobs
And Steve Wozniak,
From college dropouts
To genius founders,
From a tiny start-up in Los Altos, California,
To the first trillion-dollar Apple Inc.
The experts that offered our universe
The gift of Apple computers,
The giants alongside Microsoft and IBM
Who revolutionized the information age,
The iLife, iTunes, iMovie, iPhoto, iPod, iPhone,
A series of ingenious innovations.

Letter *B* is for Bill, Bill Gates,
The richest man on Earth,
From an argumentative child,
A tech enthusiast at the age of thirteen years,
In the limelight of Lakeside School in Seattle,
A simple, poor worker for five years,
To the youngest billionaire ever at age thirty-one,
First a dropout, then a graduate of Harvard,
The cofounder of the Microsoft Foundation,
Pledging to donate half of his wealth
Over a lifetime for good causes,
Reinventing the toilet,
Fighting poverty worldwide,
The supergood humanitarian
Who demonstrates his worthiness.

The sky has more stars
Look at other superrich people:
Jeff Bezos of Amazon;
Bernard Arnault of LVMH;
Mark Zuckerberg of Facebook;

Warren Buffett of Berkshire Hathaway;
Larry Page and Sergey Brin of Google;
Michael Bloomberg of Bloomberg LP;
The Waltons of Walmart;
Francoise Bettencourt Meyers of L'Oréal;
Mukesh Ambani of Reliance Industries Limited;
Ma Huateng of China;
Jack Ma of Alibaba;
Phil Knight of Nike;
Elon Reeve Musk of PayPal;
Colin Zheng Huang of Pinduoduo;
Aliko Dangote, the world's richest black man;
Oprah Winfrey, the world richest black woman;
Alwaleed bin Talal Al Saud, the richest Arab prince;
Sports-made billionaires Roger Federer, Cristiano Ronaldo,
Lionel Messi, Neymar, Tiger Woods, Naomi Osaka, Serena
Williams, etc.
Many more people who are superrich, not only with wealth
But also thoughtfulness.

That's one side of the mirror,
A reflection of huge wealthiness.
Turn it around, follow the arrow
To a glimpse of scientific healthiness.

Edward Jenner developed the first vaccine.
Elizabeth Blackwell, the primary female physician.
Louis Pasteur discovered that germs cause disease.
Joseph Lister pioneered antiseptic surgery
And promoted handwashing to prevent infection.
William Osler, a father of modern medicine.
Florence Nightingale, a founder of advanced nursing.
Richard M. Lawler, pioneer of organ transplantation.
Forrest M. Bird created vital respiratory ventilators.

Francis Crick, the founder of molecular biology.
Ronald Ross, the discoverer of malaria parasites.
Youyou Tu, the founder of antimalaria artemisinin.
Amitri Ivanovsky and Martinus Beijerink,
The discoverers of viruses.
William Harvey, author of *De motu cordis*,
Or *The Circulation of Blood*.
Examples of worldwide scientists
In the field of health and safety,
With fame out of selflessness.

To the needy,
Like me,
I vociferate loudly,
"Follow not
The nothingness;
Better, the wealthiness
As well as the healthiness."

A star is a star,
Whether of wealth
Or of health alone
Or even better both.
Follow nothingness;
You'll get nothing.

Target only health;
You may not afford
To fund your safety.
Kill two birds
With one stone,
Both wealth and health.
Your torch of life
Will shine brighter

And last longer
With all
That life can bring:
Happiness
And sweetness.

"Is it an egg before a chicken?"
Someone asks.
"Or a chicken before an egg?
Pick one, and the other is also right.
To say the answer is both,
The egg and the chicken,
Would it be wrong?"

It is not one or the other?
It's one, another, or both:
Wealth, health, or both
The choice is yours!

As orphans, we chose both,
Both wealth and health.
"But where will we get wealth?"
We wonder.

We can sit down here
On our poor mats,
Look at the sky above,
Choose the brightest
Twinkling star,
But how can we
Get our hands
On it?

An orphan child
Interjects,
"Let me try this:
'Oh! The super-rich!
Grant us, the poor,
Just 0.1 percent of your wealth
To complement our health,
To alleviate suffering and death,
And you'll be blessed with much more
Much more richness and happiness.'"

A child in need
Wearing rags
Joins in and asks,
"Are the needs
Of an orphan
Only two?
Wealth and health?
What about
Love
And affection?
Can money
Buy those?
I need money, I know,
But I also desire
Love and affection too."

A poet steps in.
"My pockets are empty;
Can't donate a dime to you.
Don't have a sweet voice
To stage a concert for you.
All I have is this book of poetry
To aid you."

Out there, on this planet
Are good Samaritans
Who love and care for the needy.
They may not bring your parents back to life,
May not fill your parents' shoes;
They will help you one way or another,
Fingers crossed.

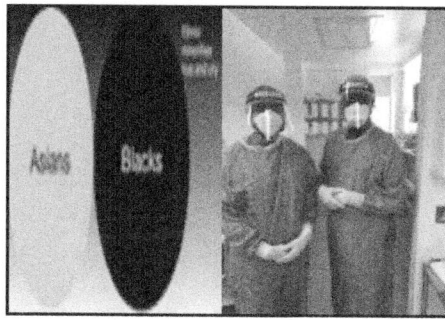

Don't Forget Us

BY ACHIER DENG AKOL

Who bleeds to death most often
During pregnancy and birth?

Who is most likely to die
From COVID-19 globally?

Who suffers most from racial discrimination
In the most developed countries worldwide?

Who is in peril of economic disaster
After the COVID-19 pandemic?

COVID-19 spares no one,
Irrespective of age and color;
Yet we, the ethnic minorities,
Bear the apex of the burden,
Be it COVID-19 or pregnancy,
Be it discrimination or poverty.

Donate to help all.
Don't forget us.

Hold Their Hands, Please, Orphans of COVID-19

BY ACHIER DENG AKOL

Weep for them, you may.
Mourn for them, you can.
Please do more for them.
Tears alone cannot save
The life of a child in need.

Weep for them, you may.
Do something beyond tears.
Please, hold the hands
Of COVID-19 orphans.

When their parents were alive,
They were able to feed,
They were able to play,
They were able to smile,
They were likely to thrive
And become future leaders,
But some are now at the risk of death.

Their parents were key workers.
They sacrificed their lives to save you
From the imminent danger of COVID-19.
They became victims of coronavirus,
Leaving vulnerable orphans so early.

Please, hold the hands
Of COVID-19 orphans.

Give Me an Ax
BY ACHIER DENG AKOL

When one enters a hall
With an overpowering smell of perfume,
People sitting close by
Will not fail to notice the smell.

When exciting news breaks
In the North Pole,
It takes but a short time to hear it
At the South Pole.

When Brazil wins a World Cup,
Football enthusiasts instantly know
And give details of how the team won,
However far they live from Brazil.

A story started in Wuhan.
A traveler relayed it elsewhere.
Another passenger took it farther.
Within weeks it spread globally.

One wishes this was a sweet story.
One would have liked it to be romantic.
But it was full of tragedy and sorrow
And provoked tears of sadness.

Distorting the beautiful word *corona*,
Adding the nasty suffix *-virus*,
Turning *la corona*, "the crown,"
Into *coronavirus*, a menace.

Give me an ax to cut off the suffix *-virus*
And leave the term *corona* without it
To save many lives in the world,
To stop the pain and sorrow of the virus.

Give me an ax!

Even an Ant Can Save Its Life

BY ACHIER DENG AKOL

To support the herd, five ants offered
To head south to lift and deliver a roll of bread.
Three of them met their fate, stepped upon by an elephant.
Trying to avoid the enormous feet of an elephant, one lost its
way.
A single ant reached the roll but could not lift the massive
treasure.

The tiny insect issued a cry for help;
The fellow herds at home were too far to hear;
Elephants continued to approach in its direction;
To dig a hole and hide was a task too late to achieve.

To fly away from the danger zone was not an option;
It had already lost its wings when it transformed into an ant.
To frighten the elephants away to change course was another
option;
This idea was nothing more than a dream for a weakling.

The sounds of the elephants' steps were getting louder and louder.
Then it noticed a gray woven thread on a wall of a house nearby.
It doubled its pace, running away from the elephants' path to hide;
While approaching the house, it became clear the thread was a spider web.

Looking behind, the vast elephants arrived on the spot.
Ahead of it, the spider was waiting in its web for prey to trap.
The expert fellow ants were too far away to offer it critical advice.
Skipping away from the path, it landed on the tail of an elephant.

The elephant's hairs trapped the ant within the tail,
And it feared the elephant would carry it too far.

It knew it was too far from its fellow ants in the hole,
And it may be taken to a strange and risky location.

It decided to tickle the skin of the elephant, who vigorously shook its tail
And threw the little ant to a haven within the neighborhood it knew.

Even an ant can save its life.

Time for Us to Compensate!

BY ACHIER DENG AKOL

I look forward to you, Friday.
From Monday to Thursday,
My eyes are on the road,
Expecting him to come.

To support us, he toils far away,
Spending the weekdays alone,
Missing us as we miss him,
A life so hard for the working class.

His clothes do not remain dirty.
I wash, iron, and pack them neatly.
His bed linens never stay untidy.
I clean and change them regularly.

When the baby cries, missing Daddy,
I soothe her with my tender voice.
When the older ones struggle with homework,
I sincerely wish he was here to help.

The sweet games couples play
Are bells that ring in my ears.
I miss my husband.
To another man, I will never turn.

For loyal wives,
Miracles indeed happen.
Lockdown to us is a miracle—
Time for us to compensate!

Be a Coronavirus Fighter

BY ACHIER DENG AKOL

Be a corona fighter.

Recovered from COVID-19?
Donate your plasma
To give antibodies.

Have funds to spare?
Sponsor a key worker
Or an orphan
Of a key worker
Who died from COVID-19.

Do something nice.
Use your funds.
Your donations
Will save lives.
Your donations

Will win the battle
Against this killer.
Save orphans of COVID-19.

Be a coronavirus fighter.

Till COVID-19 Is Crushed

BY ACHIER DENG AKOL

Wave after wave
Inflicting intense fears,
Fears followed by cries
When coronavirus smashes people.

The NHS saves.
The virus causes tears,
Tears of another demise
When immunity crashes.

Restrained like slaves,
Lockdown caused cheers
Of pleasant surprise
When pollution is slashed.

A health worker braves
The corona to up health gears,
Not surrendering
Till COVID-19 is crushed.

The Final Say Is Ours, Not Yours

BY ACHIER DENG AKOL

We defeated you before.
We will beat you again
Lock us down again sadly.
We will conquer you victoriously

We don't know you much.
We will study you thoroughly.
We will identify your weaknesses
And exploit them seriously.
We'll uncover your strengths
And counteract them vigorously.

Skip from one victim to another.
We will contact trace you farther.
Mutate to become more contagious.
We'll escalate to combat you.

Making Kazakhstan, Segriá, Leicester,
Greater Manchester, La Marina, East Lancaster,
And more regions around the globe cry again.
They will learn from their mistakes.
You now appear to be on to attacking in waves.
We ultimately will rise above you.
Come to eradicate us from our globe.
We will unanimously defeat you.

The final say is ours, not yours.

Let Us, to Nature, Be Kind
BY ACHIER DENG AKOL

The cloud above is massively bloated,
With water that dribbles
To water our crops
All over any designated farm
When the clouds are kind,
And floods that thrust downward,
Wiping away our crops,
When the clouds are angry.
Who controls the clouds?

The ocean below is deeply loaded with life.
It remains still, without waves,
Emitting only cool water droplets
To safely moisturize people around
When the sea turns a blind eye
And suddenly bursts into a tsunami,
A menace no human can stop
When the ocean is wavy.
Who controls the sea?

The wind over the sea floats.
It softly blows as it drizzles,
Gently shaking the treetops
To produce a soft sound
When the atmosphere is super fine,
And hurricanes violently gust
When the wind spares no property.
Who controls the wind?

Let us, to nature, be kind—
A lesson to keep in mind.

(Un)Happy Accident

BY PHOEBE OSARIEMEN NKECHINYERE BROBBEY

You may not know what you have given me.
While you have taken so much from so many,
You have taught me to slow down, reevaluate, and appreciate.

You have given me time to laugh and to love,
To sleep and to eat, often too much,
To see little faces grow every day,
To hold just a little longer.

You have made me glad for my life and my health.
We know so many have neither.

But you have given these gifts by a serendipitous accident.
You did not arrive to give.
You have taken, and you continue to take
Joy, time, and freedom
While you show me that my time is not mine. I will pay the
debt I accrue.

So:

I cannot say thank you.
The words stick in my throat
For those who we have lost.
I would give back all I've gained
If it meant they could feel the sun.

I will be grateful and cautious.
I will never forget.
I will give more freely, live unapologetically, but keep a piece
to myself
So that if, in my lifetime, I happen upon
Another unprecedented time,
I have something it cannot take.

Like the Parts of a Tree, We're All Connected

BY ACHIER DENG AKOL

Feed roots on one side of a tree;
They will grow and get stronger.
Leave the other roots food free;
They will become weaker.

The trunk on nourished roots
Will stand firm and straight.
Any neglected offshoots
Turn weak with less weight.

Branches over the firm trunk
Will become strong.
Branches over roots unsunk
Could break all along.

When one-half of a tree is gone
The other half might follow suit.
Charity begins at a hometown.
But all starving children need food.
Like the parts of a tree, we're all connected.

For Your Safety, We Risk Our Lives
BY ACHIER DENG AKOL

We'll continue to wear masks,
Ugly though they appear on our faces,
To protect you from a virus that is so toxic.

We will conduct risky tasks
To save your lives in critical phases,
For COVID-19 pandemic disease is so catastrophic.

We provide care when a woman in labor asks
Whether or not she has coronavirus
As dedicated caregivers,
Even though we are also scared of the virus

We turn up before long time passes,
Maintaining swift ambulance paces,
For lifesaving service is our job.
We work in the hospital day and night.

Spending a long time caring for you in various places,
Being compassionate and empathetic.

For your safety, we risk our lives.

COVID-19 Orphans

BY ACHIER DENG AKOL

When parents are alive,
They strive to exert
Efforts for children to thrive
And to avert poverty.

When a parent is dead,
There is not enough bread.
Families face destitution.
Children suffer deprivation.

For our safety,
They sacrificed their lives.
As a gratuity,
Let's support their children.

If you have a penny to spare,
Think of a COVID-19 orphan,
For their hunger pain to bear,
For a tiny slice to fry in a pan.

147

Their children's plight
Was in their mind;
Their protective fight
Was for all humankind.

With their life,
They protected everyone.
In their demise,
Let's help their little ones.

Don't Blame My Diabetes
BY ACHIER DENG AKOL

For my death, don't blame my diabetes.
I controlled it very well,
Watching my diet for decades,
Monitoring my sugar levels closely.
I was attending the diabetic clinics punctually.

Diabetes causes blindness.
I passed every eye check.
It destroys nerves and vessels.
I never felt abnormal sensations.

Till my sixties, I managed my diabetes well,
With one type of inhaler or another,
Steroids but only occasionally,
Hospital admissions very rarely.

In my sixties, I still had dreams.
I was just about to clear my mortgage,
Just about to have a grandchild,
A golden wedding anniversary underway.

Then you came and ruined everything.
You threw my dreams out the window.
A grandchild I will never hold.
A wedding anniversary cut short.

For my death, don't blame diabetes.
Blame the horrible COVID-19.
My dying wish is crystal clear:
Coronavirus, go back to hell!

The Seasons Will Change
BY AMOU TIIT AKOL TIIT

We underestimated the cold this time, so it reared its repul-
sive head.
This was no common cold, but soon it would unfold.
Our ears fall limp with exhaustion because we
force-feed them fear; now there are only knells to hear.
The strings of our masks strangle our ears
like vines, so we started strumming sweet melodies to speed
up time.
Screams are silent in the shadows of winter:
it's the darkest night of the year. The sky's
eyes are like obsidian orbs that scour the frosted
landscapes for a lost swollen sphere.

This virus does not discriminate; it's recklessly seizing lives.
But headlines tell us otherwise.
"If you're black, you're four times more likely to die"
From a virus that knows no color;
nor can it conceptualize that its repercussions intensify
economic disparities and racial disproportionalities.

Knowingly, you risk your life to protest because the seasons
will change.
Your presence was a gift to the present followed by a nod of
affirmation from the past. So ceaselessly you infatuate the
streets with your beam
as you whirl off to Battersea. COVID-19, I know you're the
enemy,
But without you many would fail to see
This nation was sick and suffering from its own disease:
An underlying rotten form of inequality.
But one thing I know about rough storms is that they ease.
Tomorrow the sun will spangle and prance, recarving the
victims' bitter, cold hearts.

The seasons will change, but will you?
If I get my foot in the door, I'll pull you through.

Things Will Be Better Again When We Beat the Coronavirus!

BY ACHIER DENG AKOL

People with comorbidities
Still made it before you arrived.
With cardiovascular disease,
Their hearts were still beating.
With chronic respiratory disease,
They continued to take their breaths.
With cancer, they still had time to live.
With diabetes, they remained stable
Until you came.

Then the world turned upside down.
The elderly were pushed into their tombs.
The weakened hearts and lungs collapsed.
You stopped everyone from breathing.

When you are gone,
Hearts will beat better again.
People will take nice breaths.
Cancer will not kill so soon.

Researchers will make breakthroughs
At Liverpool, Oxford, Harvard, and more.

Things will be better again
When we beat the coronavirus!

We Cry for You

BY ACHIER DENG AKOL

A world full of kindness
Is a world of protectors.
Occasionally it has bitterness
From a few transgressors.

Lucky you when you meet the good;
You are doomed when you meet horror.
You may eat what seems like excellent food
When an evil hand poisoned it in terror.

If you put your dirty spit
Into a tissue and then a bin
Or straight into a pit,
Not onto human skin,
You are an angel;
Otherwise, a devil.

Belly Mujinga.

We cry for you in our hearts.
The care you gave passengers
All over the underground parts,
Working tirelessly with managers.
Clients should have rewarded you.
They should not have infected you.

No one with a sound mind
Would have spat on your face
Unless his heart is so unkind.
Knowing he was a coronavirus case,
The spit would transmit the virus,
And your life would be in tatters.

A railway train worker
Spat at by a ticket dodger
Infected with the coronavirus,
Inflicting her with disease so serious,
Dying from COVID-19.
We cry for you, Miss Belly Mujinga.

Imagine!
BY ACHIER DENG AKOL

An air filter
That filters all the air
In the universe
To make it coronavirus free.

Imagine an injector in space
That injects all clouds
With a disinfectant
To wash corona off the Earth.

Imagine a vacuum
That sucks away germs
Out of hospitals, nursing homes,
Leaving them coronavirus free.

Imagine a magnifying glass
That magnifies viruses into giants
All over the atmosphere
To see, dodge, and smash.

157

Imagine magnetic trees
That can grasp coronaviruses
And convert them into useful oxygen
Via virus-to-oxygen metamorphosis.

Imagine commensal viruses
That outmaneuver coronaviruses,
Depriving them of room to multiply
To prevent them and protect humans.

Imagine absorbent footballs
That absorb coronavirus from the air.
Let professional footballers dribble them away
And kick them up to hell to burn there forever.

Imagine!

Who Will Pull Me Out?

BY ACHIER DENG AKOL

You abandoned me for another man
When things were a little brighter.
You took away my motivation
When we had a chance to make it.

Now I have sunk deeper
Into painful misery,
Into extreme poverty.
Things may never be better.

Yes, I earned a PhD
After you abandoned me.
Of what use is it now
At the fragile age of sixty-six?

My love pigeon
Trying to fly back to me
After I released her,
To prove she is truly mine.

But in a hole of shame,
In a mess of poverty,
In a sea of financial debts,
In an ocean of problems.

Who will pull me out of these holes?
To receive, hold, and hug you.
To taste your sweetness again.
To welcome you back.

Who will pull me out?

Buried Again in Burton

BY ACHIER DENG AKOL

Two little ones suffering with me
In the absence of their caring mother.
My specialty training program, ruined.
An opportunity to become a consultant, foiled.

Buried before in Harrow
With debts up in the air.
A Mercedes car, given up
A large house, repossessed.

One hand cannot clap itself.
One hand trying to make it
In the City of Birmingham,
Caring for kids and working.

The other hand in London,
Struggling to make it there
Away from her little ones,
Refusing to join her husband.

Now, in the second life in Burton,
Raising four late-arriving kids,
Commuting distances for work,
Sponsoring new love in my life.

Loans building up again,
Debts only the tip of the iceberg.
A mortgage yet to clear,
Sliding back into a grave.

Buried again in Burton.
Leave Nuneaton alone.

If Money Grew on Trees

BY ACHIER DENG AKOL

If money grew on trees
Like branches and leaves,
I would be a millionaire
And possibly a billionaire.

The single apple tree
In my back garden
Instills hope in me.
If money grew on trees.

If I counted the leaves
On the lawn and trees
In my house's back garden,
They could be thousands.

If every leaf
Represented a fifty-pound note,

Multiplying thousands by fifty pounds,
I would climb the ladder of wealth.

If money grew on trees.

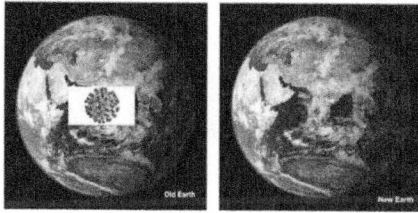

To Grapple with You

BY ACHIER DENG AKOL

Coronavirus!
Have you come to live with us
On this Earth?
We will ask God
To create another Earth
Solely for us.

The new Adam and Eve
Will sin no more
In a second garden,
Having learned serious lessons.

Let God transfer good people,
The kindhearted,
The innocent lovers,
To live on the new Earth
Away from the horrible you.

As for criminals,
The dreadful sinners,
The terrible offenders
Remain on the old Earth
To grapple with you.

No Soap Left to Spare

BY ACHIER DENG AKOL

A cock crowed twice.
The dawn has emerged.
A morning breeze so nice,
I fetched a broom.
It's time to work before sunrise,
Sweeping, brushing, washing, cleaning
To give our parents a sweet surprise.
We learned excellent things from them."

A cool breeze after the rain
Softly touching our skin,
Blowing away any bitter pain.
We will ultimately win.

Drops of dew on the grass,
Glistening and gliding softly.
Spectacular views that outclass
All its natural rivals.

Oh! The sun is about to rise.
A little piece of soap to share.
Need to wash my hands twice.
There is no soap left to spare.

No soap left to spare.

Corona Came to the Countryside; It Found Our Morale High

BY ACHIER DENG AKOL

All around us is green.
It is the rainy season.
Crops, including beans,
We farm for a reason.

The sorghum is white.
The pumpkin is yellow.
The sweetcorn is bright.
Food to soon swallow.

All around us is blue,
The lakes with clear waters
That you can look through
To spot fishes in colors.

Astonishing butterflies,
Many marvelous flowers,
A wonderful bird cries—
All that nature empowers.

All around us is calm
With no traffic hustle,
Less crime and harm
Without urban bustle.

Corona came to the countryside;
It found our morale high.

The Water We Fetch Stops the People from Catching Coronavirus
BY ACHIER DENG AKOL

Young as we are,
We go to fetch water
From wells so far,
Whatever the matter.

We meet friends and chat
All along our route.
We may stagger and pant.
We'll each earn a fruit.

Dad clearing a farm,
Mum plucking and cooking,
Boys sounding alarms—
Everyone is up and working.

Who else will fetch water?
A grandmother that is so frail?
Who will instead stagger?
A grandpa that can't see the trail?

171

The water we fetch
Stops the people from catching the coronavirus.

Which One Should We Kill, Coronavirus or Our Culture?

BY ACHIER DENG AKOL

Our culture of generosity,
Nothing can override it.
The spirit of solidarity
Will help us to get rid of coronavirus.

Giving water to drink,
Feeding the guests,
Serving without a blink
As generous hosts.

The cornerstones of our culture
For generations after generations.
No one will alter its structure
Without receiving condemnations.

We share water from a family pot,
A risky practice during the pandemic.
Let's wash cups and leave no spots
After sharing water with guests.

Which one should we kill,
Coronavirus or our culture?

Let Us Social Distance in and around a Dance Floor

BY ACHIER DENG AKOL

After dinner is over,
We're full of energy,
The moon shining brighter—
Bless us, oh clergy

The sound of African drums
Resonating profoundly in the air,
Alerting every youth to jump,
A cultural dance to dare.

Girls pick gents to pair
The most handsome and the best dancers,
Those gents they can share love with,
Their potential future life partners.

The excitement begins before the dance,
With courtship around the dance floor.
The fun will not end when the dance stops.

They accompany lovers to their doors.

We will sit far from one another
During this phase of courtship.
We won't dance close to each other,
Two meters from other's hip.

This event is not just courting;
It allows vital connection.
It is not pure dancing;
It allows partner selection.

Let us social distance
In and around a dance floor
Till coronavirus is all over.

Not without Network

BY ACHIER DENG AKOL

During the lockdown,
I felt loveless.
Like someone who's drowned,
I felt lifeless.

Where there is no Facebook,
Where there is no Twitter,
No telephone and phone book,
Loving in lockdown is harder.

No more romantic visits,
Even with parental permission.
It's all travel limits
Without romantic exemptions

Forget about hugs,
Not to mention kisses.
There are fewer thugs,
One of the corona blisses.

Comfort on FaceTime.
Utilize your Skype.
Phone every time.
On the keyboard, type.

Not without network.

Coronavirus, Please, Don't Touch Our Cattle!

BY ACHIER DENG AKOL

A beautiful sunset on the Nile.
Time for cattle to return home
After grazing for a long while.
At night, cattle should not roam.

Herds of cattle returning
To the lads, a sign of success,
The lactating cows mooing,
Milk for the calves in excess.

The cattle tied to wooden pegs,
Smoke fire lit in the middle
To chase mosquitoes and ticks
So the cattle do not wriggle.

A herd of your own is a pride,
A symbol of a wealthy status
To pay as dowry for a bride,
A valuable marriage impetus.

Milk, yogurt, cheese, butter
Cow dung, a natural soil fertilizer
Skin, hide, beef, bones, ploughing
Essentials for economic security.

Coronavirus, please,
Don't touch our cattle!

Worry about Corona Later

BY ACHIER DENG AKOL

A person hit by a vehicle,
An individual caught in a fire,
A child drowning in a river,
A wife attacked by a lion,
A pregnant woman bleeding,
A patient having a heart attack,
People trapped in earthquake,
Others struck by a volcano.

When danger threatens a life,
Rescue the person in danger.
Help the person to survive.
Worry about corona later.

More than Coronavirus

BY ACHIER DENG AKOL

Yes! COVID-19
Is fatal
And quite global,
A danger for sure,
But there are more.

Malaria, cholera, meningitis
Pregnancy, and gastroenteritis—
Look at the infant mortality.
Take a glance at maternal mortality.

In sub-Saharan Africa
Nationally and regionally.
In Asia and South America
Globally, internationally.

Not your country.
You may pay for a trip.

Not your county.
To you, it may slip.

Coronavirus is not the only killer.
Let's not loosen our grip on others.
COVID-19 is undoubtedly a danger.
Do not relax the care of pregnant mothers.

There are more dangers than coronavirus.

No Rules to Break

BY ACHIER DENG AKOL

Nature fills the lake with fish.
They are ready to be harvested.
An elder issues the order
To those who are interested.

People choose a date for harvesting.
Everyone gets the nets ready.
To go there alone is cheating.
Check that your basket is steady.

They sound a trumpet.
Crowds from all directions emerge
With nets and baskets mounted;
They head to the lake to converge.

Smiling, singing, laughing, fishing—
No quarrels or disputes allowed.
Carrying, packing, loading, catching—
With abundant fish, they go home proud.

They can social distance in a lake,
With no community rules to break.

Let Me Not Cry; My Turn Will Come
BY ACHIER DENG AKOL

I have mixed feelings.
I am left home alone.
They took my siblings
To school after dawn.

Have I done something wrong?
Am I not a good lad?
Haven't we been off school too long?
How long shall we stay sad?

Let me not cry.
The PlayStation is all mine.
Instead, let me try
To excite my mind.

All computer entertainment,
The entire big-screen television,

All the kitchen refreshments
Are fully mine while I'm in seclusion.

Let me not cry;
My turn will come.

My Little Child Maa-Adut Will Not Accept

BY ACHIER DENG AKOL

We did not build
Our beautiful world
And lovely cities
For you to destroy.

You, the venomous,
crushing our health.
You, the disastrous,
ruining our wealth.

Children of the world,
Leaders of tomorrow
Will not accept.

In the center of the Earth,
In the heart of London
They stood proudly
To denounce you.

Our little daughter
Maa-Adut
Will not accept
Stretching her arms
To cover the globe.
She earnestly strives
To protect the world.

New York will survive.
Kuajok will continue to grow.
Wuhan city will thrive.
London will continue to glow.
Mumbai will remain alive.

Look!
Vaccination has started
To mark the beginning
Of your end

Destroy our world
And our cities? No!
My little child Maa-Adut
Will not accept.

Era Three:
A New World–after Corona

Hooray! Hooray! Hooray! Football Is Back, Anyway!

BY ACHIER DENG AKOL

Hooray! Hooray! Hooray!
Football is back live.
Horse racing is underway.
Rugby will soon arrive.

Stadium seats may be empty.
Fans will fill them up again,
Now watching afar in plenty.
The leagues have restarted.

The photo of a football manager
In the middle of the empty seats—
A powerful worldwide message,
A reminder that corona still beats.

Listen to the sound of jubilation,
The cheers after a match is won.
Feel the silence of humiliation,
The tears of bitter loss and lash.

A team may have lost a game.
Sports have reclaimed their fame.
Coronavirus will go in shame,
The germ that holds the blame.

Hooray! Hooray! Hooray!
Football is back, anyway!

What a Life We Have Missed!

BY ACHIER DENG AKOL

Shopping centers have reopened.
Nothing saved while on furlough
Will purchase a pantie as a token
To lift my heart from sorrow.

Nonessential goods, they were called.
Was that phrase not wicked?
With no pants, shoes, and clothes sold,
Wouldn't people be walking naked?

Mothers, dust the pushchairs.
Strap in your little ones.
It's time to breathe fresh air
During vibrant shopping runs.

In pushchairs, babies are excited,
Smelling a McDonald's meal.

In rows, people queue open-minded,
Staring at essentials offered with a deal.

What a life we have missed!

Our Lives Will Again Be Better

BY ACHIER DENG AKOL

A surprise on the horizon:
The spectrum of a rainbow
Over the back garden,
A ray of hope to follow.

The hope we need
To see a brighter future
After a successful beating
Of the coronavirus killer.

A sign of good things
To come
After all the bad ones
Are overcome.

This virus will be history.
It will not kill us any longer.
Let's not worry so much.
Our lives will be better again.
Our lives will be better again.

Farming: An Essential Requisite / For the Weak

BY ACHIER DENG AKOL

A family recently bereaved,
A neighbor that has died,
An elderly that is diseased,
A disabled person without sight.

Unable to hold a hoe,
We cannot effectively cultivate
With no crops to sow.
We will ultimately have no food.

A future looks bleak
With no grain to deposit.
Farming, for the weak:
An essential requisite.

Able men volunteer
To sow, weed, and harvest.
Women brew beer
To reward them in earnest.

Farming: an essential requisite
For the weak.

We Have Had Enough
BY ACHIER DENG AKOL

All of a sudden, we lost everything.
Sadly, we remained with nothing.
A killer appeared from somewhere.
It aggressively spread everywhere,
Our lives and economy destroyed,
Even with protective measures deployed.

In the past, it was a Spanish virus;
Yesterday it was ebolavirus;
Recently it has been a coronavirus.
Tomorrow, which?

No more.
No more viruses.
We have had enough.

Don't Come Again, You Filthy Sludge!

BY ACHIER DENG AKOL

If you come again,
You will find us ready.
You'll not catch us by surprise
Like you did to us before,
You filthy sludge.

Should you come back,
We'll beat you again,
Faster and tougher.
Do not forget the lesson
We have taught you.

If you dare come again,
We'll beat you swiftly
Now that we all know
How horrible you are.
Coronavirus! COVID-19!

Don't come again,
You filthy sludge!

Health and Safety's Prayer

BY ACHIER DENG AKOL

Oh! God!
Oh! Lord!
You, we praise;
Us, you raise.

Protect our health;
Prevent our death
From epidemics
And pandemics,
From attackers
And murderers.

Amen.

We Have Moved On; Let's Not Stride Back

BY ACHIER DENG AKOL

Sociologists say
At the beginning, when we lived in the forests,
The strongest bull controlled the entire herd
And had all the heifers to himself.
No other bull was allowed to climb on a heifer.
The bulls fought one another every day,
Killing themselves for the right to have all
The girls and women in the human herd.

Men were dying, bull after bull.
The women decided to take matters up,
To be the ones to pick as many bulls as they liked,
To have her, in turn, without grumbling.

Polyandry, this was called,
Done to rescue the lives of their men,
Lest they finished killing one another,
Lest there would be no man left.

The control shifted from bulls to cows,
And the bulls were twitchy about this.
They agreed to stop killing one another.
A man should pick as many heifers as he liked,
Peacefully, without bloodshed,
Without crossing openly to others' wives.
A new rule called polygamy dawned—
With so many heifers, no need for bloodshed.

Sexually transmitted diseases were rampant.
One man infected so many women
He did not even know their names.
In the old Sudan, a man had ninety-nine wives.

People considered monogamy to be safer.
The human folk adopted it unanimously.

Now, my husband, tell me,
Why do you want to wind the clock back?

Who is that woman you visit secretly?
Was she locked down with you?
When I am stranded overseas,
Would you like me to do the same?
To have another man secretly, too,
To enjoy myself with others too?

Why do you want to rewind the clock,
To the dark old days of polygamy,
To the horrible era when the strongest bull owned all?
Have you forgotten there was also polyandry?

Why do you want to rewind the clock

To the miserable times of coronavirus?
Don't you know we are living during triumphant times?

Why do you want to rewind the sociology clock?

During These Straying Times

BY ROBY SHAMAS

An unhinged virus leaves me
Besieged
By the sobering uncertainty
Of the unknown,
Enveloped in this
Unrecognizable,
Groundless
Blur.
Fast-forward, I cannot.
So, I retreat,
Shelter in place.
I allow in the worst of it,
Tune in to the whole of it,
Hold what I can bear.
As for the rest?
I'll take a loan out of time
And ration it with the wind.

When did that old normalcy
Wither away and disappear?
And when will the new one begin?
My malleable memory tells me,
"It once was clear,"
And my comforting mind says,
"It's meant to be…"
"Just ask the unwavering stars,"
They both echo back to me.
Oh, I know.
My cold intellect is not medicine;
My internal story holds that cure.
But mine is a wandering mind.
So I allow myself to rest in it
And drift away.
And from behind
The safety of these blinds
And a private vision,
This multicentered life
Unfolds before my eyes:

A child innocently wonders:
"Are we all being grounded?
When will my life begin?"
A frightened parent sighs,
Projecting her fears:
"Oh, how I wish I knew about days like these."

A man

Bound to meet his agency
On an undetermined date
Doesn't notice himself saying:
"For now,

I will hold and wait,
Wait for the ground
To land beneath our bare feet again
And for the times of certainty to return."

A poet turns inward
To feel the words
That tether him to his inner light,
His sanity, today:
It's a time out of time,
A time that cares less for reason or rhyme,
A time that tests our perseverance and resilience,
A time that exposes our need for convenience,
Time to, again, appreciate the touch,
A time to get by without much,
A time for adults to self-soothe with theories,
Time to binge on TV series,
A time to lend space for what matters to materialize,
A time for the terrifying deniers to minimize,
A time to rush to reclaim the illusion of control
And to recover that familiar, old role,
A time to have the excess shed,
Time for our Earth to self-mend,
A time for the trees in the woods to have an undisturbed
dialogue,
A time to eavesdrop on that internal monologue,
Time for the rocks to welcome the moss,
A time for us to reconcile with the loss
And to slowly, very slowly, recognize the gravity of that
bind—
Time, not yet ready to be defined
Nor foreseen.

An intellectual's mind strays
Into yet another meditation,
Reciting,
To no one in particular,
A lecture the day before his life began:
"Forget not
That from where you stand,
Your life always extends
Between recalling the beginnings
And repressing the inevitable end,
And its center
Will always land at the place we call
'Here.'"

On the window of my home,
A quote read:
"My life begins when I can feel the now."
I look closer,
At my own reflection in the window
And try to hold my gaze,
But I'm always looking away
With a smirk that says "because I can..."

My Heart Still Beats for You, Darling J

BY ACHIER DENG AKOL

Our ages have ticked away.
We have become elderly and frail,
Our feet at the edge of the grave.
I feel for you even more.

They replaced my hip bone,
But I remain intimately yours.
Your love still flows in my blood.
You still rule my brain and nerves.

Water dribbles from me
And the cream, too, occasionally.
The heat of your love
Makes me sweat time after time.

My heart still beats for you, Darling J.

Wrong words like *F*s and *S*s
Never slipped from our lips.

"Loml" and "Darling J," our terms,
"Love of my life" and "Darling Jo."

My aged and feeble arms
Can be blown by the wind.
Still, I can stretch them around you
Close enough to feel your heartbeat.

It's incredible how time flies.
Seventy-five years ago, we tied the knot.
Now, over ninety, we still sit side by side,
Like teenage Romeo and Juliet.

Nothing under the sun and the moon
Will ever come between you and me,
Not even coronavirus and death.
My heart still beats for you, Darling J.

When the time comes for us to go,
Given our sinless hearts and skins,
Our mortal souls will continue to shine,
Corona free in the heaven above.

My heart still beats for you, Darling J.

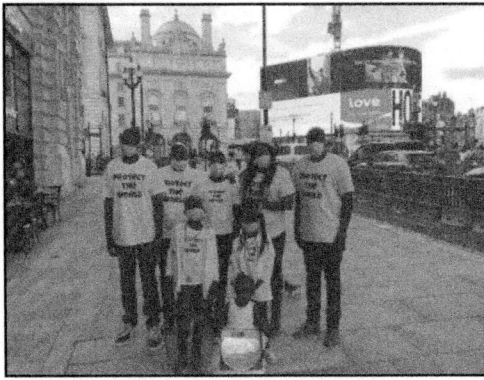

Protect the World

BY ACHIER DENG AKOL

A poem from the perspective of a one-year-old child, called Maa-Adut

At my tender age of one year,
My hands around the globe,
I say to all, "Don't worry.
All will be well."

Almighty God above,
My family behind me,
I stand proud and strong
In the center of the world.

For the sake of children like me,
For everyone on this globe,
I plea with my feeble lips,
"Protect the world."

My early dreams are raw
Beyond the breast milk,
Besides my mum's hug,
Yet I aspire for the best.

The best for me and you,
The best for the future to come,
The best for our health and safety,
For the young and old,
For the able and disabled.

Protect the world.

Printed in Great Britain
by Amazon